VERONICA RUFF

After the Funeral

A Christian Companion Guide for the First Year of Grief

Contents

After the Funeral

A Christian Companion Guide for the First Year of Grief

After the Funeral

A Christian Companion Guide for the First Year of Grief

Veronica Ruff

Integrity Press Publishing

Dedication

For those who are walking through the quiet days after loss.
May these pages bring comfort, peace, and the gentle reminder that you are not alone.

Introduction

Grief often becomes most real in the days after the funeral.

In the quiet moments that follow, when the visitors have returned home and life begins to move forward again, many people find themselves facing a new and unfamiliar landscape. The house may feel different. Ordinary routines may carry a deeper silence. Small moments can suddenly remind us of the person we love and miss.

This companion has been written for those early months of grief, when the heart is learning to live with loss.

Each chapter offers a short reflection on experiences that many grieving people encounter during the first year after the death of someone they love. These reflections are accompanied by Scripture and simple prayers that can be read whenever comfort or reassurance is needed.

You may wish to read the book slowly, returning to particular chapters when certain moments arise. There is no right pace for grief, and no expectation that every page must be read in order.

The hope of this book is simply to offer quiet companionship along the way — a reminder that grief is a natural expression of love, and that God remains close to the brokenhearted.

May these pages bring you moments of peace as you walk through the first year of grief.

I

The First Days

When the House Feels Different

Sometimes the reality of loss does not fully settle in at the hospital, or even during the funeral.

In those moments there are often many people around. Doctors and nurses move through quiet corridors. Family members gather close. There are conversations, decisions, and arrangements to be made. Everything can feel strangely suspended, as though time itself has slowed.

For many people, the moment when grief becomes most real is when they return home.

The door opens to familiar rooms. The furniture is in its usual place. Everyday objects sit quietly where they have always been. Yet something feels different.

The house may seem unusually still.

You might find yourself listening for a voice that once filled the room. Perhaps your eyes drift toward a chair where they often sat, or you notice something small that belonged to them. In these gentle but painful moments, the heart begins to understand what the mind already knows: life has changed.

This experience can feel deeply heavy. Coming home may make the loss feel more real than it has before.

Yet these moments also reveal something profound. The quiet of the house speaks of a life that was deeply present within it. The routines, the laughter, the familiar sounds of daily living—all of these were woven into the rhythm of the home.

Grief often appears in these ordinary places because love once lived there so fully.

If the house feels different now, it is because the life that filled it mattered deeply.

In time, the spaces that now feel quiet may slowly begin to hold memories as well as sorrow. The chair, the room, the familiar corners of the home may become places where gratitude for a life shared begins to grow alongside grief.

For now, it is enough simply to acknowledge the heaviness of this moment.

God understands the sorrow that settles quietly in the heart.

Scripture reminds us:

"The Lord is close to the brokenhearted

and saves those who are crushed in spirit."

— Psalm 34:18

Even in the quiet of a changed home, you are not alone.

Prayer

Lord,

In the stillness of this home,

be near to my heart.

Hold me gently in this grief,

and bring your peace into the quiet spaces.

Amen.

The Quiet After the Funeral

In the days leading up to a funeral, there is often much to do.

Family members gather. Arrangements must be made. There are conversations with funeral directors, decisions about readings and music, and the steady arrival of visitors offering their support. During this time, grief can sometimes feel held within the activity that surrounds it.

Then the funeral takes place.

Words are spoken. Prayers are offered. Memories are shared. Friends and family come together to honour the life of the person who has died.

But after the funeral, something changes.

The visitors slowly return to their homes. The phone begins to ring less often. Messages become fewer. The world gently resumes its normal rhythm.

And suddenly, there is quiet.

For many people, this is when grief begins to feel more present. Without the structure of arrangements and gatherings, the heart may finally begin to absorb what has happened.

This quiet can feel unfamiliar and heavy.

You may notice how still the days feel. Simple routines may carry a new weight. Moments that once seemed ordinary can now feel strangely different.

It is important to remember that this quiet is a natural part of grief.

When the activity surrounding loss fades, the heart begins its slow work of mourning.

There is no need to rush this process.

Grief does not follow a timetable, and there is no correct pace for healing. Some days may feel manageable, while others may feel unexpectedly difficult.

In these quiet days, be gentle with yourself.

Allow space for rest. Allow space for tears. Allow space for the memories that may surface when the world grows still.

God is present not only in moments of strength, but also in moments of silence.

Scripture reminds us:

"Be still, and know that I am God."

— Psalm 46:10

Even when the house is quiet and the days feel long, God remains close.

Prayer

Lord,

In the quiet days after loss,

stay near to me.

Help me to find rest in your presence

and comfort in your peace.

Amen.

When Grief Comes in Waves

Grief rarely moves in a straight line.

Some days may feel calm and manageable. You may find yourself able to move through familiar routines, speak with others, or even experience moments of quiet peace.

Then, without warning, a wave of grief can rise.

It may come through a memory, a photograph, a familiar place, or a song that suddenly brings the person you love vividly back to mind. At other times the wave may seem to come for no clear reason at all.

These moments can feel overwhelming.

The heart may suddenly feel heavy. Tears may come unexpectedly. A deep longing for the person who has died may fill the moment with sorrow.

Experiences like this are a natural part of grief.

Love does not simply disappear when someone dies. The bond that was formed through years of shared life continues to live in the heart. Because of this, memories and emotions can surface in powerful ways.

It can sometimes help to imagine grief as the tide of the ocean.

There are moments when the water feels calm and distant, and moments when the tide rises and moves close to shore again. Neither experience is wrong. Both are part of the natural rhythm of grief.

When these waves come, it may help to pause and breathe slowly. Allow the feeling to move through the moment rather than trying to push it away.

Over time, many people find that the waves become less overwhelming. They may still come, but they often arrive with a gentler rhythm.

For now, it is enough simply to recognise that what you are experiencing is part of loving someone deeply.

Scripture reminds us that God is present even in moments of emotional storm.

"God is our refuge and strength,

an ever-present help in trouble."

— Psalm 46:1

When grief rises unexpectedly, you can rest in the assurance that God walks beside you through every wave.

Prayer

Lord,

When waves of grief rise within me,

be my refuge and strength.

Help me to find steadiness in your presence

and comfort in your care.

Amen.

When the Body Feels Tired

Grief does not only affect the heart and mind.

It can also touch the body in quiet but powerful ways.

In the days and weeks after a loss, many people notice an unusual tiredness. Even simple tasks may feel heavier than they once did. You may find yourself needing more rest, or feeling as though your energy disappears quickly.

This kind of exhaustion can be surprising.

Grief asks much of the human heart. Emotions rise and fall, memories surface, and the mind is slowly learning to adjust to a new reality. All of this quiet work can leave the body feeling worn and fragile.

At times you may feel as though you should be stronger, or that you ought to return to your normal pace of life. Yet grief rarely moves according to our expectations.

It is important during this season to allow yourself the grace of rest.

Sleep when your body asks for it. Move gently through your days. Accept help when it is offered. These small acts of care are not signs of weakness; they are part of allowing the heart and body to heal.

Just as a physical wound requires time to mend, the wounds of loss also need patience and kindness.

Even Jesus understood the need for rest during times of sorrow and strain. Scripture often reminds us that God cares for our whole being— body, mind, and spirit.

"The Lord gives strength to his people;
the Lord blesses his people with peace."
— Psalm 29:11
When weariness comes, remember that it is not a failure. It is simply part of the journey of grief.

Be gentle with yourself in these days.

Prayer

Lord,

When my body feels weary

and my strength is low,

grant me rest and quiet renewal.

Help me to move gently through this season

held in your peace.

Amen.

When the World Keeps Moving

One of the strange experiences of grief is the way the world continues as though nothing has changed.

Cars move along familiar roads. Shops open their doors each morning. People go to work, meet friends, and carry on with their daily routines. Life continues with its usual rhythm.

Yet inside your heart, something profound has shifted.

You may find yourself looking around and wondering how everything can appear so normal when your own world feels so different. The loss of someone deeply loved can make ordinary life feel almost unreal for a time.

This feeling is very common in grief.

When someone who has been an important part of your life is no longer present, the change can feel enormous. Your heart is adjusting to a new reality while the rest of the world continues on its familiar path.

At times this difference can feel lonely.

You may feel as though others cannot fully understand the weight you are carrying. Even when people offer kindness and sympathy, there can still be moments when grief feels deeply personal and quiet.

During these times, it may help to remember that grief does not need to match the pace of the world around you.

There is no need to hurry your healing or pretend that everything feels normal again. Grief has its own rhythm, and it unfolds slowly in its own time.

As the days pass, you may gradually find moments when the world feels a little more familiar again. Small routines may return, and life may slowly begin to take shape in new ways.

Until then, it is enough simply to move gently through each day.

God sees the quiet struggles of the heart, even when they are invisible to others.

Scripture reminds us:

"The Lord himself goes before you and will be with you;

he will never leave you nor forsake you."

— Deuteronomy 31:8

Even when the world moves forward, you are not walking through grief alone.

Prayer

Lord,

When the world seems to move on

while my heart is still grieving,

stay close beside me.

Give me patience with myself

and remind me that you walk with me each day.

Amen.

II

The Moments That Make It Real

The Empty Chair

Grief often appears in quiet and unexpected moments.

It may come when you enter a familiar room and notice something small that has changed. Perhaps your eyes rest on a chair where someone once sat, or on a place at the table that now remains empty.

These moments can arrive suddenly.

You may pause for a moment, remembering the conversations that once took place there. The laughter, the everyday stories, the simple presence of the person who used to sit in that place.

An empty chair can speak very loudly to the heart.

It reminds us that someone who was once part of our daily life is no longer physically present. What once felt ordinary now carries a deep sense of absence.

These experiences are a natural part of grief.

Love leaves its mark on the spaces we share. The places where we gathered, spoke, and lived together hold memories that remain long after someone is gone.

Seeing that empty chair may bring sadness, but it also reflects the depth of the relationship that once filled that space.

The love that existed there has not disappeared.

Over time, many people find that these places begin to hold not only sorrow but also gratitude for the life that was shared. The chair that now feels empty may one day become a quiet reminder of the many moments of love that happened there.

For now, if the sight of that empty place brings tears, allow them to come.

Grief is simply love that continues to remember.

Scripture offers this gentle assurance:

"Blessed are those who mourn,

for they will be comforted."

— Matthew 5:4

God sees the quiet sorrow that can arise from the simplest reminders.

Prayer

Lord,

When small reminders bring grief to my heart,

help me to remember the love that was shared.

Hold my memories gently

and comfort me in the quiet moments.

Amen.

Reaching for the Phone

There may come a moment when you instinctively reach for the phone.

Perhaps something happens during the day that you would normally share with the person you love. It might be good news, a small story, or simply the familiar desire to hear their voice.

Without thinking, your hand moves toward the phone.

Then the quiet realisation returns.

They are no longer there to answer.

Moments like this can feel deeply painful. What was once an ordinary habit suddenly becomes a reminder of loss. The simple act of making a call now carries the weight of absence.

These experiences are very common in grief.

The routines we share with those we love become woven into our daily lives. For many people, phone calls were part of that rhythm— quick conversations, small updates, or the comfort of hearing a familiar voice.

When someone dies, those patterns do not disappear immediately. The heart remembers the connection that once existed, even when the mind already understands the loss.

If you find yourself reaching for the phone and feeling that sudden wave of sadness, know that this moment is a reflection of love. It shows how naturally that person belonged within your everyday life.

Over time, the sharpness of these moments may soften. The memory of those conversations may begin to bring warmth as well as sorrow.

For now, allow yourself to feel whatever the moment brings.

God understands the quiet ache that can arise from the smallest habits of love.

Scripture reminds us:

"The Lord is close to the brokenhearted

and saves those who are crushed in spirit."

— Psalm 34:18

Even in moments when the silence feels heavy, God remains near.

Prayer

Lord,

When familiar habits remind me of the one I miss,

comfort my heart.

Hold my memories gently

and surround me with your peace.

Amen.

Hearing a Familiar Voice

Sometimes grief appears in the most unexpected ways.

You may hear a voice in another room that sounds like the one you loved. Perhaps someone laughs in a familiar way, or speaks with a tone that suddenly reminds you of them.

For a brief moment, your heart may pause.

It may feel as though the person you lost is still nearby, just out of sight. The thought can arrive quickly and quietly before the mind remembers the truth.

They are no longer here.

Moments like this can feel confusing and emotional. The heart may leap forward with recognition before the mind has time to understand what has happened.

Experiences like this are very common in grief.

When someone has been part of our daily life, their voice, their expressions, and the way they spoke become deeply familiar to us. These memories live strongly within the heart and mind.

Because of this, hearing something similar can awaken the memory of their presence very quickly.

While these moments can bring sadness, they also reveal something beautiful about the depth of our connection. The voice you remember was once part of your everyday life. It became woven into the sounds and rhythms of your home and your memories.

Grief sometimes echoes through those familiar sounds.

Over time, hearing a voice that reminds you of the person you love may begin to bring gentle memories along with the sorrow.

For now, if the moment catches your heart by surprise, know that this is a natural part of remembering someone deeply loved.

God understands the quiet emotions that can arise from these simple reminders.

Scripture offers this assurance:

"The Lord is near to all who call on him,

to all who call on him in truth."

— Psalm 145:18

Even when memories appear unexpectedly, God remains close.

Prayer

Lord,

When memories return through familiar sounds,

bring peace to my heart.

Help me to hold these memories with love

and rest in your presence.

Amen.

The Day You Almost Call Their Name

There may come a moment when you almost call their name.

Perhaps you are moving through the house and instinctively begin to speak to them, just as you always did. It might be a simple question, a small comment, or a familiar phrase that once belonged to everyday conversation.

For a brief second, it feels natural.

Then the quiet truth returns.

They are no longer there.

Moments like this can feel deeply painful. The words may stop halfway, and the silence that follows can feel heavy. What was once part of the ordinary rhythm of life suddenly becomes a reminder of loss.

These experiences are very common in grief.

When someone has shared our daily life, speaking to them becomes second nature. We ask their opinion, share small moments, or simply say their name without thinking.

Those habits of love do not disappear overnight.

The heart continues to remember the relationship that once filled those ordinary moments. In many ways, these experiences reveal how naturally the person belonged within your life.

If you find yourself almost calling their name, allow yourself a moment of gentleness.

There is nothing unusual or wrong about these experiences. They simply reflect the deep connection that once existed between you.

Over time, the sharpness of these moments may soften. The memory of their name may begin to bring warmth alongside the sorrow.

For now, if tears come, allow them.

Grief is the heart's way of honouring love.

Scripture offers this promise:

"Blessed are those who mourn,

for they will be comforted."

— Matthew 5:4

God sees the quiet moments when the heart remembers.

Prayer

Lord,

When I remember the voice and name

of the one I love,

hold my heart gently in your care.

Let their memory remain a blessing

and bring comfort to my soul.

Amen.

When Memories Appear Without Warning

Grief often carries memories with it.

Sometimes those memories arrive gently, when we choose to look at photographs or think about the past. At other times, they appear suddenly and without warning.

You may be driving along a familiar road, preparing a meal, or walking through a place you have visited many times before. Then something small—a sound, a smell, a place, or a passing thought—brings a memory vividly back to mind.

For a moment, it may feel as though time has folded back on itself.

You might remember a conversation, a shared laugh, or a simple moment that once seemed ordinary. The memory can feel so real that it stirs both warmth and sadness at the same time.

Experiences like this are a natural part of grief.

When someone has been deeply woven into our lives, their presence becomes part of the memories we carry. The mind and heart hold countless moments that once formed the everyday story of your relationship.

Because of this, memories may appear unexpectedly.

Sometimes they bring comfort. Other times they may bring tears. Both responses are part of remembering someone who mattered greatly to you.

Over time, many people find that these memories begin to feel less overwhelming. What once caused sudden sorrow may slowly become a source of gratitude for the life that was shared.

For now, if a memory stops you in the middle of an ordinary moment, allow yourself a pause.

These memories are a reflection of love that has left its mark on your life.

Scripture reminds us that love itself is a gift that endures.

"And now these three remain: faith, hope and love.

But the greatest of these is love."

— 1 Corinthians 13:13

Even as memories rise and fall, the love that created them remains part of your story.

Prayer

Lord,

When memories return suddenly,

help me to receive them with gentleness.

Hold my heart in your peace

and let love remain stronger than sorrow.

Amen.

Seeing Something They Would Have Loved

Grief sometimes appears in the middle of ordinary moments.

You might see a place, a view, or something small during the day that immediately makes you think of the person you miss. It could be a favourite meal, a familiar song, a joke they would have laughed at, or something beautiful that you wish you could show them.

For a moment, your first instinct may be to share it.

You may find yourself thinking, *They would have loved this.*

Then the quiet truth returns.

They are no longer here to see it.

These moments can bring a sudden wave of sadness. The desire to share life with someone we love is one of the most natural parts of being human. When that person is gone, those small opportunities to share can feel painfully empty.

Yet these moments also reveal something meaningful.

They show that the person you loved continues to live within your thoughts and your awareness of the world. The things that mattered to them, the way they saw life, and the joy they found in simple moments remain part of the way you experience the world.

In this way, love continues to shape the heart even after loss.

When you notice something they would have loved, it may help to pause for a moment and quietly remember them. The beauty you see can become a gentle reminder of the life you shared together.

Over time, these moments may begin to feel less like absence and more like quiet remembrance.

Scripture reminds us that love leaves a lasting imprint on the heart.

"Above all, love each other deeply,

because love covers over a multitude of sins."

— 1 Peter 4:8

Even when someone is no longer beside us, the love we shared continues to influence the way we see the world.

Prayer

Lord,

When something reminds me of the one I love,

help me to hold that memory with gratitude.

Let the love we shared continue to bring light

even in moments of sorrow.

Amen.

Opening the Wardrobe

There may come a day when you open a wardrobe or drawer that has remained closed since the loss.

Inside are the familiar things that once belonged to the person you loved. Clothes still hang where they were placed. A jacket rests over a hanger. Perhaps there are shoes, scarves, or small personal belongings arranged just as they were left.

For a moment, time may seem to stand still.

These items carry a quiet presence. They remind us of the life that once moved through the home — the routines of getting ready for the day, the familiar habits of dressing, the ordinary moments that once felt so natural.

Opening that space can bring a sudden wave of emotion.

The reality of loss may feel very close in that moment. Something as simple as a coat or shirt can hold memories of shared days, conversations, and everyday life together.

There is no right or wrong way to respond to these moments.

Some people choose to leave these belongings untouched for a time. Others may eventually feel ready to sort through them slowly. Each person moves through this part of grief in their own way and at their own pace.

What matters most is allowing yourself the freedom to move gently.

If opening that wardrobe brings tears, let them come. These objects carry the quiet story of a life that mattered deeply.

In time, these belongings may become reminders not only of loss but also of the love and memories that remain.

Scripture reminds us that the love we share is never lost.

"Let all that you do be done in love."

— 1 Corinthians 16:14

Even in the small things left behind, the story of love continues.

Prayer

Lord,

When familiar things remind me of the one I miss,

comfort my heart.

Help me to hold these memories with tenderness

and peace.

Amen.

When They Appear in a Dream

During times of grief, many people experience dreams that feel especially vivid.

In these dreams, the person who has died may appear clearly. They may look peaceful, healthy, or simply present in a familiar way. Sometimes they speak. At other times they may simply stand nearby or share a quiet moment.

When you wake, the dream can remain in your thoughts for a long time.

These experiences can feel deeply emotional. For some people they bring comfort. For others they may stir both peace and sadness together. The feeling of seeing someone who has been lost, even within a dream, can touch the heart in a powerful way.

Dreams have always been part of the mysterious way the mind and heart process life.

During grief, the memories and emotions we carry often become especially present. Because of this, it is not unusual for the people we love to appear in our dreams.

For many grieving individuals, these dreams bring a gentle sense of reassurance. They may awaken with a feeling of calm, as though for a brief moment the distance between memory and presence has grown smaller.

However these experiences are understood, they often remind us of something important: love does not disappear.

The relationship we shared with the person who has died continues to live within our memories, our hearts, and the story of our lives.

If you experience dreams like this, receive them gently. They may simply be part of the heart's way of remembering someone deeply loved.

Scripture reminds us that God remains present even in the quiet places of the night.

"When you lie down, you will not be afraid;

when you lie down, your sleep will be sweet."

— Proverbs 3:24

Even in sleep, God holds the heart with care.

Prayer

Lord,

When memories of the one I love

appear in quiet moments or dreams,

bring peace to my heart.

Let love remain stronger than loss

and rest gently in your presence.

Amen.

III

Walking Through Grief

The Weight of Loss

Grief can sometimes feel like a quiet weight carried within the heart.

In the early days after loss, the mind may still be adjusting to the reality of what has happened. As time passes, the full depth of the absence can begin to settle more deeply into everyday life.

Many people describe this experience as a heaviness.

Simple tasks may feel more difficult than they once did. Conversations may require more effort. Even ordinary routines can feel slower and more demanding.

This weight is not something that others can always see.

From the outside, a person may appear to be managing their days as usual. Yet inside, the heart may still be carrying the deep awareness that someone dearly loved is no longer present.

This quiet burden is a natural part of mourning.

Grief asks the heart to slowly learn how to live in a world that has changed. The love that once flowed through daily life must now find a new place to rest within memory and remembrance.

This adjustment takes time.

If the weight of grief feels heavy on certain days, allow yourself the kindness of patience. There is no need to rush the healing of the heart.

Just as physical wounds require time to mend, the wounds of loss also require gentleness and care.

God understands the burdens that are carried quietly within us.

Scripture offers this invitation:
"Come to me, all you who are weary and burdened,
and I will give you rest."
— Matthew 11:28
Even when grief feels heavy, you are not meant to carry it alone.
Prayer
Lord,
When the weight of grief feels heavy upon my heart,
help me to rest in your care.
Carry what I cannot carry alone
and give me strength for each new day.
Amen.

When Questions Come

Grief often brings questions.

In the quiet moments of reflection, the mind may begin to search for meaning or understanding. You may find yourself wondering why this loss happened, why it happened when it did, or why life sometimes unfolds in ways that feel so difficult to accept.

These questions are a natural part of grief.

When someone we love dies, the heart tries to make sense of a change that feels overwhelming. It is human to look for explanations, to revisit memories, and to wonder whether things might have been different.

Sometimes the questions have no clear answers.

In these moments, it is important to remember that asking questions does not mean that faith has disappeared. Even people of deep faith have struggled with uncertainty during times of sorrow.

Throughout Scripture we see examples of faithful people who brought their questions to God. They spoke honestly about their confusion, their pain, and their longing for understanding.

God welcomes that honesty.

Faith does not require that we have every answer. Instead, faith often means continuing to trust God's presence even when life feels difficult to understand.

If questions arise in your heart, allow them to exist without fear. They are part of the mind's way of processing loss and searching for meaning during a painful season.

Over time, the heart often discovers that while not every question receives a clear answer, God's presence remains steady.

Scripture reminds us:

"Trust in the Lord with all your heart

and lean not on your own understanding."

— Proverbs 3:5

Even when life feels uncertain, God continues to walk beside you.

Prayer

Lord,

When questions fill my mind

and understanding feels distant,

help me to rest in your presence.

Give me peace in the unknown

and guide my heart through this season.

Amen.

Grief and Faith

For many people, grief touches not only the heart but also their faith.

In times of loss, faith can feel both comforting and challenging at the same time. You may find moments when prayer brings peace, and other moments when your heart feels quiet or uncertain.

This is a very natural experience.

When someone we love dies, the depth of the loss can stir many emotions. The heart may move between trust and sadness, hope and confusion, strength and vulnerability. Faith does not remove these feelings; instead, it walks with us through them.

There is no need to pretend that grief is easy.

Throughout Scripture we see that people who loved God deeply still experienced sorrow and struggle. The Psalms are filled with honest expressions of grief, longing, and questions directed toward God.

Faith does not mean that pain disappears.

Rather, faith reminds us that even in the midst of pain, we are not alone. God understands the depth of human sorrow and remains close to those who mourn.

If your faith feels strong on some days and fragile on others, know that this too is part of the journey of grief. Faith often grows quietly during the most difficult seasons of life.

God's presence does not depend on the strength of our feelings in any given moment.

Scripture offers this reassurance:
"The Lord is close to the brokenhearted
and saves those who are crushed in spirit."
— Psalm 34:18
Even when faith feels quiet or uncertain, God remains near.
Prayer
Lord,
When grief touches my faith
and my heart feels uncertain,
help me to trust in your presence.
Strengthen my spirit
and remind me that you walk beside me always.
Amen.

When Prayer Will Not Come

There may be moments in grief when prayer feels difficult.

You may sit quietly, wanting to pray, yet find that the words do not come. Your heart may feel tired, numb, or overwhelmed. Even the familiar prayers that once felt natural may seem distant.

This experience is more common than many people realise.

Grief can affect the whole person—heart, mind, and spirit. When the weight of sorrow feels heavy, it is not unusual for prayer to feel different for a time.

Some people worry that this means their faith has weakened.

But the absence of words does not mean the absence of faith.

Sometimes the deepest form of prayer is simply being present before God, even in silence. God understands the emotions that cannot easily be spoken. He sees the sorrow that lives quietly within the heart.

The Bible reminds us that even when we struggle to find words, God still hears the prayers of the heart.

"We do not know what we ought to pray for,

but the Spirit himself intercedes for us

through wordless groans."

— Romans 8:26

In other words, when we cannot pray, God still understands.

If prayer feels difficult in this season, allow yourself the grace of quiet presence. Sitting silently before God can be its own form of prayer.

There will be time again for words.
For now, it is enough simply to rest in God's care.
Prayer
Lord,
When I do not know how to pray
and words feel far away,
receive the quiet of my heart.
Stay close to me in this season
and hold me gently in your peace.
Amen.

When Anger Appears

Grief can stir many different emotions.

Alongside sadness, there may also be moments of frustration or anger. These feelings can sometimes surprise us, especially if we believe that grief should only be expressed through sorrow.

You may feel angry about the circumstances surrounding the loss. You may feel frustration that life has changed in ways you did not choose. At times, anger may even appear without a clear reason.

These emotions are not unusual.

Loss disrupts the life we once knew. The heart is trying to adjust to a reality that feels painful and unfair. In that process, strong emotions can naturally rise to the surface.

Some people feel uneasy when anger appears during grief. They may worry that such feelings are wrong or that they reflect poorly on their faith.

But emotions themselves are not a failure of faith.

Throughout Scripture we see people expressing deep honesty before God. The Psalms include moments where grief, frustration, and confusion are spoken openly. God welcomes that honesty because it reflects a real relationship.

If anger arises in your heart, allow yourself to acknowledge it without fear. Bringing those feelings to God can be part of the healing process.

Over time, many people find that these emotions gradually soften as the heart continues to heal.

God remains present through every part of the journey, even the moments when emotions feel complicated.

Scripture reminds us:

"The Lord is compassionate and gracious,

slow to anger, abounding in love."

— Psalm 103:8

God understands the depth of human emotion and meets us with patience and compassion.

Prayer

Lord,

When strong emotions rise within me,

help me to bring them honestly before you.

Guide my heart toward peace

and surround me with your compassion.

Amen.

When You Feel Alone

Grief can sometimes feel like a very lonely journey.

Even when people around you care deeply and offer support, there may still be moments when the loss feels intensely personal. The person you loved shared a unique place in your life, and no one else can fully understand that relationship in the same way.

Because of this, there may be times when you feel alone with your grief.

The world around you may continue moving forward. Friends and family may gradually return to their normal routines. Yet the space left by the person you have lost remains deeply present within your heart.

This difference can sometimes create a sense of quiet isolation.

It is important to remember that feeling alone in grief does not mean that you truly are alone.

Many people walk this same path of mourning, each carrying their own story of love and loss. Although every experience of grief is unique, the journey itself is shared by countless others who have loved deeply.

Most importantly, God remains present in every moment of sorrow.

Even when the heart feels isolated, God sees and understands the quiet burdens that are carried within us. His presence does not depend on whether we feel strong or steady on a particular day.

Scripture offers this comforting assurance:

"Even though I walk through the darkest valley,

I will fear no evil, for you are with me."

— Psalm 23:4

These words remind us that God walks beside us even in the most difficult seasons of life.

If grief ever feels lonely, take comfort in the knowledge that God's presence is constant. He remains close to the brokenhearted and faithful through every step of the journey.

Prayer

Lord,

When grief makes me feel alone,

remind me that you are near.

Surround me with your presence

and bring comfort to my heart.

Amen.

IV

The Year of Firsts

The First Birthday Without Them

Birthdays often carry joyful memories.

They are days when we celebrate the life of someone we love. In past years there may have been phone calls, messages, shared meals, or quiet moments of recognition that marked the day as special.

After a loss, the first birthday without that person can feel very different.

The day may arrive with a quiet awareness that something important has changed. You may find yourself remembering how birthdays were once celebrated or recalling small traditions that belonged to that day.

These memories can bring both warmth and sadness.

It is natural to feel the absence more strongly on days that once held meaning. The heart remembers the way life used to be and recognises that something precious is now missing.

There is no single way to move through this day.

Some people choose to quietly remember the person who has died. Others may light a candle, say a prayer, or spend time reflecting on the life that was lived. Some may prefer to keep the day simple and gentle.

Whatever you choose, allow yourself the freedom to honour the day in a way that feels right for you.

The love that once celebrated those birthdays has not disappeared. It remains part of your story and continues to shape the memories you carry.

Scripture reminds us that every life is known and valued by God.
"Teach us to number our days,
that we may gain a heart of wisdom."
— Psalm 90:12
Even as time moves forward, the life of the person you love remains precious in God's sight.

Prayer

Lord,
On this day that once held special meaning,
hold my memories gently.
Help me to remember the life I loved
with gratitude and peace.
Amen.

The First Christmas

For many families, Christmas is a time filled with tradition.

Homes are decorated. Familiar meals are prepared. Carols and gatherings bring people together in celebration. The season often carries memories of shared joy, laughter, and time spent with those we love.

After the loss of someone dear, the first Christmas can feel very different.

You may notice their absence in ways that feel especially tender. Perhaps there is a place at the table that now sits empty, or a tradition that reminds you strongly of the person who is no longer there.

Moments that once brought simple joy may now carry both warmth and sadness.

These feelings are completely natural.

Christmas is a season that celebrates love, family, and togetherness. When someone important is missing, the heart naturally feels that absence more deeply during these moments.

It is important to allow yourself gentleness during this time.

Some people choose to keep familiar traditions, while others adjust them or create new ways of remembering the person they love. Lighting a candle, sharing stories, or simply speaking their name can be meaningful ways of honouring their memory.

At the heart of Christmas is the message that God came near to a world that often feels fragile and broken.

Even in seasons of grief, that message remains.

Scripture reminds us:

"The light shines in the darkness,

and the darkness has not overcome it."

— John 1:5

The presence of sorrow does not erase the light of hope.

Even in a Christmas touched by grief, God's love remains steady and near.

Prayer

Lord,

During this season of remembrance and celebration,

comfort my heart.

Help me to hold both memory and hope together

and fill this time with your peace.

Amen.

The First Family Gathering

Family gatherings often carry deep meaning.

They are times when people come together to share meals, stories, and the familiar rhythms of being with one another. These moments can feel comforting because they remind us of the connections that shape our lives.

After the loss of someone dear, the first family gathering can feel very different.

You may notice their absence in small but powerful ways. Perhaps there is a seat that once belonged to them, a conversation that reminds you of their voice, or a moment when you instinctively expect them to be part of the gathering.

These moments can stir both warmth and sadness.

Family gatherings often carry shared memories, and those memories may feel especially close when everyone is together again. It is natural to feel the absence of someone who once helped shape those moments.

Some people worry about how they will respond during these gatherings. They may wonder whether they will feel overwhelmed with emotion or uncertain about how to talk about the person who has died.

There is no single way to experience these moments.

You may find comfort in sharing memories, or you may simply wish to listen quietly as others speak. Both responses are part of honouring the life that was shared.

Being together as a family can also be a reminder that love continues to surround us, even in times of grief.

Scripture offers this reassurance:

"Bear one another's burdens,

and so fulfill the law of Christ."

— Galatians 6:2

God often brings comfort through the presence and care of others.

Prayer

Lord,

As family gathers and memories return,

help us to hold one another with kindness.

Let love guide our conversations

and bring comfort to every heart.

Amen.

The First Anniversary of Their Passing

As the months pass, certain dates begin to approach quietly on the calendar.

One of the most significant can be the first anniversary of the day your loved one died. When that day arrives, it may bring a deep awareness of the journey you have walked through during the past year.

You may find yourself remembering the events of that day very clearly.

The mind may return to the hospital, the conversations that took place, or the moments when you first realised that life had changed. Memories that have softened over time may feel vivid again for a while.

This experience is very common.

Anniversaries have a way of gathering memories together. They remind us not only of the day itself, but also of the love, the life, and the journey that followed.

You may also notice how much you have carried through this past year.

There may have been days of deep sorrow, moments of unexpected strength, and times when quiet memories brought comfort. The path of grief is rarely simple, but every step reflects the love that remains within the heart.

Some people choose to mark this day in a gentle way.

You might light a candle, say a prayer, visit a meaningful place, or spend a quiet moment remembering the person you loved. These small acts can be a way of honouring both the life that was shared and the journey that continues.

Scripture reminds us that God's compassion remains steady through every season.

"Because of the Lord's great love we are not consumed,

for his compassions never fail.

They are new every morning."

— Lamentations 3:22–23

Even on days that carry deep memories, God's presence remains constant.

Prayer

Lord,

On this day of remembrance,

hold my heart with compassion.

Help me to honour the life I loved

and continue forward in your peace.

Amen.

Visiting Their Resting Place

There may come a day when you visit the place where your loved one now rests.

For some people this may be a cemetery or memorial garden. For others it may be a place where ashes were scattered or somewhere that held special meaning in the person's life.

Approaching that place can bring many emotions.

You may feel a quiet heaviness as you arrive. Standing there may make the reality of loss feel very close again. At the same time, it can also be a moment of reflection and remembrance.

Many people find themselves speaking quietly during these visits.

You might share a thought, say a prayer, or simply stand in silence. These moments can feel deeply personal, as though the bond of love continues even though life has changed.

It is important to remember that the resting place is only one part of the story.

The life you shared with the person you loved is not contained within that place. Their memory lives within your heart, within the memories you carry, and within the ways their love has shaped your life.

For some people, visiting their resting place becomes a quiet tradition—a way of pausing to remember and honour the life that was lived. For others, these visits may be occasional and reflective.

There is no single way to approach these moments.

What matters most is allowing yourself to remember with gentleness and respect for the journey you have walked.

Scripture reminds us that the love we share is held within God's care.

"He will wipe every tear from their eyes.

There will be no more death or mourning

or crying or pain."

— Revelation 21:4

These words offer the promise that sorrow is not the final chapter.

Prayer

Lord,

As I remember the one I love,

fill my heart with peace.

Help me to honour their life with gratitude

and rest in the hope you provide.

Amen.

V

Holding On to Hope

Love Does Not End

Grief is often described as the price we pay for love.

When someone we love dies, the relationship we shared does not simply disappear. The daily presence may be gone, but the love that shaped the relationship continues to live within the heart.

This is one of the quiet truths of grief.

The bond that was formed through years of shared experiences, conversations, and memories remains part of who we are. Love leaves a lasting imprint on our lives.

In the early days of loss, the absence can feel overwhelming. The heart may focus mainly on what has changed and what has been lost. Yet over time, many people begin to notice something else as well.

Love continues.

It lives in the stories we remember, the values that were shared, and the ways the person we loved shaped our lives. The kindness they showed, the lessons they taught, and the moments you shared together all remain part of your journey.

In this way, love does not end with death.

Instead, it changes form. What was once expressed through daily presence becomes a quiet memory carried forward in the heart.

For many people, recognising this truth brings a gentle sense of comfort. The relationship may no longer exist in the same way, but the love that created it remains.

Scripture reminds us that love itself is one of the most enduring gifts God has given.

"And now these three remain: faith, hope and love.

But the greatest of these is love."

— 1 Corinthians 13:13

Even in the midst of grief, love continues to speak through memory and gratitude.

Prayer

Lord,

Thank you for the love that I shared

with the one I miss.

Help that love to remain a blessing

within my heart and my life.

Amen.

Remembering Their Life

As time passes, grief slowly begins to change.

In the early days after a loss, the heart often feels the sharpness of absence. The mind returns again and again to the moment when everything changed. The sorrow can feel close and constant.

Yet over time, something gentle often begins to happen.

Memories of the life that was shared slowly begin to come forward alongside the sadness. The mind remembers conversations, laughter, familiar routines, and the small moments that once formed everyday life together.

These memories are part of the story of love.

They remind us that the person we lost was not defined only by the moment of their passing, but by the life they lived and the relationships they built. Every act of kindness, every shared meal, every conversation contributed to the story that now lives in memory.

Remembering someone's life can become a meaningful way of honouring them.

Some people share stories with family and friends. Others look through photographs, revisit places that were important, or quietly reflect on the lessons they learned from the person they loved.

These acts of remembrance help keep the story of a life alive.

In time, many people find that remembering brings not only tears but also gratitude. The sorrow of loss may remain, but it is joined by appreciation for the years and moments that were shared.

Scripture reminds us that every life is known and valued by God.

"The memory of the righteous is a blessing."

— Proverbs 10:7

The life you remember continues to have meaning and influence.

Prayer

Lord,

Thank you for the life of the one I loved.

Help me to remember their story

with gratitude and peace,

and let their memory remain a blessing.

Amen.

Carrying Their Legacy Forward

Every life leaves a legacy.

The people we love shape us in ways that often continue long after they are gone. Through their words, their values, and the way they lived, they leave quiet influences that become part of our own story.

In the early days of grief, it may feel difficult to think about the future.

The heart may still be adjusting to the absence of someone who once shared the journey of everyday life. Yet as time passes, many people begin to notice that the influence of the person they loved continues to live on.

Perhaps it appears in the way you treat others with kindness, remembering how they once showed compassion. Perhaps it appears in a habit, a tradition, or a simple phrase that still echoes in your thoughts.

These small things are part of the legacy they leave behind.

Carrying that legacy forward does not mean forgetting the loss. Instead, it means allowing the goodness of their life to continue shaping the world around you.

Every act of kindness, every moment of generosity, every word of encouragement can reflect the influence of the life you shared with them.

In this way, their story continues.

Scripture reminds us that a life lived with love and faith leaves lasting fruit.

"Let your light shine before others,
that they may see your good deeds
and glorify your Father in heaven."
— Matthew 5:16
When you carry forward the values and love you shared, the influence of that life continues to bring light to others.
Prayer
Lord,
Thank you for the life and influence
of the one I loved.
Help me to carry forward the goodness
they shared with the world
and let their legacy continue through love.
Amen.

When Joy Returns

At some point during the journey of grief, a moment of joy may quietly return.

It might arrive in a simple way—a shared laugh with a friend, a peaceful walk, a beautiful view, or a small moment of happiness that appears unexpectedly during the day.

When this happens, some people feel surprised.

Alongside the joy, another feeling may appear: a quiet sense of guilt. You may wonder whether it is right to feel happiness again when someone you love is no longer here.

These feelings are very common.

Grief often carries a deep sense of loyalty to the person who has died. Because of that love, it can sometimes feel as though allowing joy means leaving the memory of that person behind.

But this is not the case.

The return of joy does not erase love or diminish the significance of the person you lost. Instead, it reflects the natural way the heart slowly learns to carry both memory and life together.

Love and joy can exist alongside remembrance.

The person you loved was part of your life, and the love you shared helped shape who you are. That love does not disappear when you begin to smile again.

In many ways, allowing moments of joy honours the life that was shared. It reflects the goodness, kindness, and happiness that once existed within the relationship.

Scripture reminds us that God walks with us through both sorrow and renewal.

"Weeping may stay for the night,

but rejoicing comes in the morning."

— Psalm 30:5

These words offer the gentle assurance that grief does not have the final word.

Prayer

Lord,

When moments of joy return,

help me to receive them with peace.

Remind me that love remains

and that life can continue to grow

alongside memory.

Amen.

Until We Meet Again

Grief reminds us how deeply we are capable of loving.

When someone we cherish dies, the separation can feel painful and difficult to understand. The absence may remain present in many quiet moments, even as time continues to move forward.

Yet within the Christian faith, grief is held alongside hope.

The Bible speaks often of God's promise that death does not have the final word. For those who trust in Him, life continues beyond what we can see. The love we shared is not lost, and the story of our lives does not end with earthly farewell.

This promise does not remove the sadness of parting.

It is natural to miss the voice, the presence, and the everyday companionship of the person who is gone. Grief reflects the depth of that love.

But alongside the sorrow, there remains a quiet hope.

The Christian faith teaches that one day there will be reunion in the presence of God. The separation that feels so painful now will not last forever. The promise of eternal life reminds us that love belongs to a story larger than the years we share on earth.

Until that day, the memories we carry continue to honour the life that was lived.

The love you shared remains part of your heart, your story, and the journey you continue to walk.

Scripture offers this comforting promise:
"And so we will be with the Lord forever.
Therefore encourage one another with these words."
— 1 Thessalonians 4:17–18
These words remind us that hope remains even in the presence of loss.
Prayer
Lord,
Thank you for the love I shared
with the one I miss.
Help me to walk forward with hope,
trusting in your promise
that love and life continue in you.
Amen.

Prayers for Difficult Days

A Prayer When Grief Feels Heavy

Lord,

Some days grief feels heavier than I expect.

Memories return suddenly, and the absence of the one I love feels very close. In these moments, help me to remember that you see my sorrow and understand my heart.

Give me strength for this day.

Hold me in your compassion.

And remind me that I am not alone.

Amen.

A Prayer When Memories Feel Overwhelming

Lord,

Today my thoughts are filled with memories of the one I miss.

Some memories bring comfort, while others bring sadness. Help me to receive them gently, without fear.

Let the love we shared remain a blessing in my life.

Bring peace to my heart and quiet to my mind.

Amen.

A Prayer for the Night

Lord,

As night falls and the world grows quiet, my heart sometimes feels the weight of loss more deeply.

Be near to me in these quiet hours.
Calm my thoughts and bring rest to my spirit.
Let your presence surround me with peace as I sleep.
Amen.

A Prayer When Loneliness Appears

Lord,

There are moments when grief feels lonely.

Remind me that you are near even when my heart feels empty. Help me to trust that your presence surrounds me and that your love remains constant.

Fill the quiet spaces with your comfort.

Amen.

A Prayer for Strength

Lord,

As I continue walking through this season of grief, grant me strength for each new day.

Help me to move forward gently, carrying both memory and hope. Guide my heart with your wisdom and surround me with your peace.

Amen.

Scriptures for Comfort and Hope

During seasons of grief, many people find strength in returning to Scripture. These passages offer reminders of God's presence, compassion, and promise of hope even in the midst of sorrow.

You may wish to return to these verses whenever you need reassurance or quiet encouragement.

The Lord Is Near
"The Lord is close to the brokenhearted
and saves those who are crushed in spirit."
— Psalm 34:18

God Walks With Us
"Even though I walk through the darkest valley,
I will fear no evil, for you are with me."
— Psalm 23:4

God Carries Our Burdens
"Come to me, all you who are weary and burdened,
and I will give you rest."
— Matthew 11:28

God's Peace
"Peace I leave with you; my peace I give you.
Do not let your hearts be troubled."

— John 14:27

Nothing Can Separate Us From God's Love
"For I am convinced that neither death nor life…
will be able to separate us from the love of God."
— Romans 8:38–39

God's Compassion Is New Each Day
"Because of the Lord's great love we are not consumed,
for his compassions never fail.
They are new every morning."
— Lamentations 3:22–23

Hope Beyond Sorrow
"He will wipe every tear from their eyes.
There will be no more death or mourning or crying or pain."
— Revelation 21:4

Also by Veronica Ruff

Integrity Press Publishing

Other titles by Veronica Ruff include:

Choosing Meaningful Funeral Readings, Prayers and Hymns

A Simplified Catholic and Christian Guide for Families Making Decisions Under Pressure

A Cosy Easter Table

Simple Recipes for Family, Friends, and Easy Hosting

The Easter Colouring and Activity Book

A Gentle Collection of Easter Puzzles, Colouring Pages, and Reflections

The Easter Devotional

40 Days of Prayer, Reflection, and Family Devotions for Lent and Easter

When Work Becomes War

Healing from Workplace Bullying and Betrayal

For more resources and upcoming titles from Integrity Press Publishing, visit:

https://linktr.ee/integritypresspublishing

About the Author

Veronica Ruff is the founder of Integrity Press Publishing and the author of a growing collection of faith-based and reflective works designed to offer encouragement, guidance, and comfort during life's most meaningful seasons.

Her writing focuses on Christian living, grief support, prayer, and thoughtful reflection. Through gentle and accessible writing, she aims to create resources that help readers navigate difficult moments while remaining grounded in faith and hope.

Many of her books are written to support individuals, families, churches, and pastoral care communities, particularly during times of loss, transition, and spiritual reflection.

Veronica believes that words can offer quiet companionship during life's hardest seasons, and her work is dedicated to providing readers with thoughtful, faith-centred resources they can return to whenever comfort and reassurance are needed.

More books and resources from Integrity Press Publishing can be found at:

https://linktr.ee/integritypresspublishing

A Small Request

If this book brought you comfort or encouragement during your time of grief, I would be grateful if you would consider leaving a brief review where you purchased it.

Reader reviews help others who may be walking through a similar season find resources that offer support and hope.

Thank you for taking the time to read this book, and may you continue to find peace and comfort in the days ahead.